FROM THE OUTSIDE

A visual journey to Glastonbury Festival

Nick

All the best

Karen 21/4/14

Laura J Zaky

Foreword by Michael Eavis

First Edition October 2013

Copyright © 2008-2013 Laura J. Zaky

Photography Laura Zaky
Design Matt Bone
Copyright © p11&12 Oska Zaky out of the car shots
Copyright © p46 Morgan Zaky Waterfall of light

British Library Cataloguing-in-Publication Data.
A catalogue record for this book is available from
the British Library

Published by Osmo Publishing
mail@laurazaky.com

Printed in Glastonbury, UK by Direct Offset

ISBN 978-0-9927068-0-7

Michael

Glastonbury Festival has grown from its humble beginnings in 1970, from a gathering of a few thousand people on a couple of fields, to the size it is today.

The Festival's links with Glastonbury itself go back to the middle ages when Worthy Farm belonged to Glastonbury Abbey. The monks built one of their finest Tithe Barns here, in our fields at Pilton which is retained in all its magnificence to this present day.

At its heart are the people who come to make the world's largest greenfield performing arts festival. The festival goers, stall holders and sizeable staff come together to spend a few days a year to create that unique Glastonbury experience.

This book is a photographic record of some of the bands, performers, workers and festival goers who have helped to make the festival a very special place to visit.

I hope Laura's photographs take you on a visual journey into the Glastonbury Festivals over recent years and may yet inspire some of you to come or become more involved in what I believe is one of the best Performing Arts Festival in the world.

Photographer

I love people, expressions of our passions and desires in what we do.... Moments in time captured forever...

Inspired to show my children how not just to sit about and do nothing. If you want something go out and get it, be part of it. Use what you have; talent, drive, emotion and your instincts. Also to give something back. I wanted to prove to them that if you have a dream a dream it can be reality.

I am donating 50% of the profits to Glastonbury Abbey for their Save our Ruins appeal & GFM Glastonbury's radio station. It's a Glastonbury thing!

I dedicate this book to my amazing father Harold for always believing in me and supporting me, my late mother Betty and my incredible children Oska & Morgan for putting up with their bonkers mum!

Thank you to: Michael Eavis for writing the foreword, all the sponsors who have adverts in the back of the book that enabled this to be printed.
Thank you to: Jason, Matt (for your awesome design work!), Ali, Pat, Avia, AGC, Kim, Bruce and all of you who enjoy and have supported my work. Thank YOU!

www.laurazaky.com

FROM
THE
OUTSIDE

Sid from Cbeebies

Glastonbury pre-festival

Festival goers arrive in

First Great Western at Castle Cary. An amazing collaboration of services. Ensuring the smooth running of the trains and getting the festival goers through swiftly and safely.

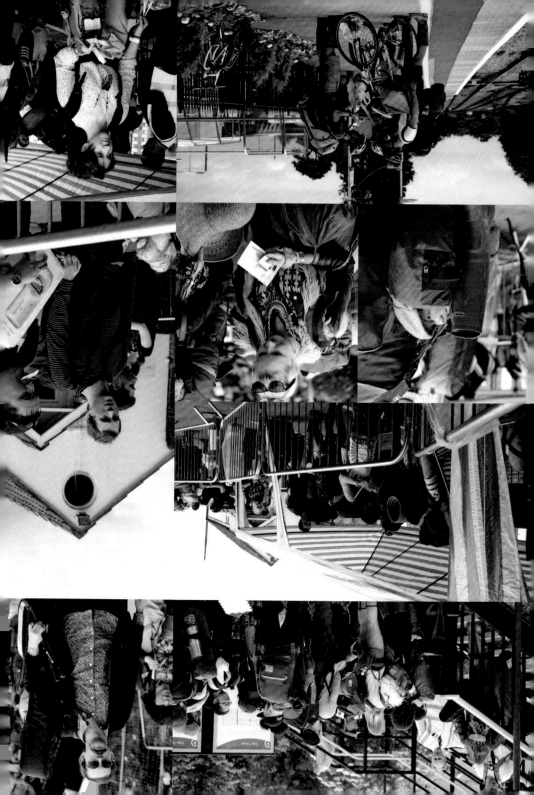

The AA

The fourth emergency service. The VW camper was being towed to site with a stop off at Morrissons for supplies.

The Police

Have a slick operation at the festival working from two sites. Using bikes, horses, bicycles, officers etc. Keeping the festival a safe place to be and also in the spirit of things!

NI

His Royal Highness
the Prince of Wales
at Glastonbury visiting
the Greenpeace area during
the 40th year celebrations
at Glastonbury Festival

Recycling is a big thing at Glastonbury. A massive operation of around 1,700 people who service the whole site during the festival. There is a team that work for 2 weeks to clear the site back to mother nature ready for the cows to return.

GET
ON
MY
LAND!

Michael is a people person. Always engaged always interested. Never seen in trousers rain or shine, shorts are his unique identifier alongside a wide smile and a quick chat along the way.

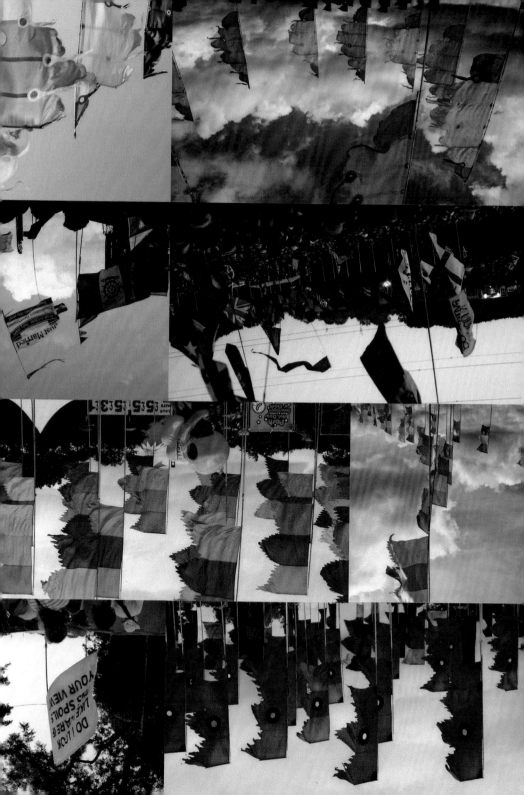

Banksy @ Glastonbury

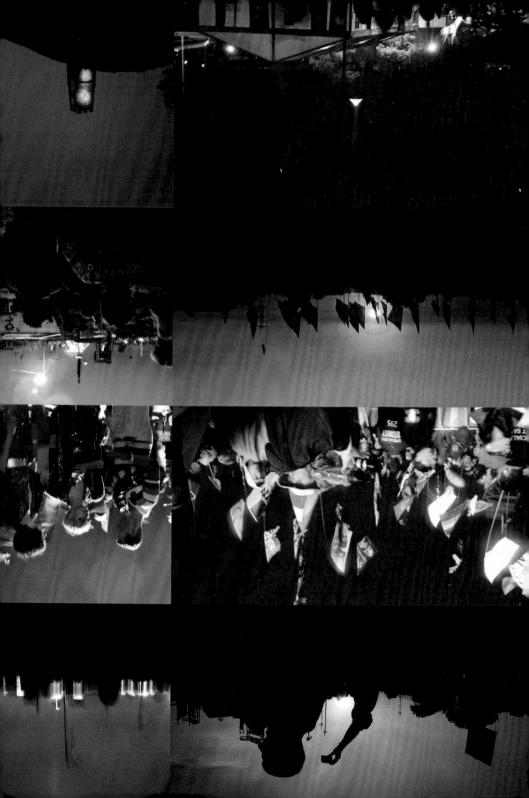

Sponsors

Glastonbury Ales, Burns the Bread
Overlook B&B / Dicketts Art Shop
Glastonbury Post Office
JJ's Taxis
Mocha Berry Café

THANK YOU

To the sponsors who have made the printing of this book possible.
We hope that when you visit **Glastonbury** you will pop in and see them.
Do listen in to GFM on 107.1FM and visit the beautiful Glastonbury Abbey,
both of these worthy causes will benefit from the sale of this book.

BURNS THE BREAD

ANYBODY'S BUTTER

BUT BURNS THE BREAD IS BEST!

Our range of breads, besides the traditional of white, wholemeal and malted grain, include: French Grain, Pecan Nut, Walnut, Multi-seed Sourdough, Pumpkin Seed, Seeded Country Cob with Sourdough, Sunflower Seed, Bavarian Rye, Spelt, Spelt and Rye, Soda Bread.

There is a selection of sandwiches and filled rolls daily. Our Savouries include our best seller the Glastonbury pasty, as well as our Veggie pasty. Sausage rolls, Cheese and Onion, Broccoli and Cheese slices. Quiches come in slices or you can buy them whole. We pride ourselves on the wide variety of 'naughty but nice' cakes and pastries that include the old favourites such as do' nuts, Chelseas, Danish pastries etc etc.

We provide delicious, freshly prepared buffets for any occasion, including Board meetings, Weddings, Parties, Christenings, Funerals or any other event that requires high quality buffet food.

01458 831532 14 High Street, Glastonbury, BA6 9DU
www.burnsthebread.co.uk

Also located in St Dunstans Car Park next to Glastonbury Abbey

01458 831645 Unit 12 01458 448181 Street 01963 350779 Castle Cary 01749 677779